From Africa
to the Present
Thank You
for the Music

From Africa
to the Present
Thank You
for the Music

Margaret L.J. McCants

Illustrated by Alicia W. Simon

Thank You for the Music & More
From Africa to the Present

Written by Margaret L. J. McCants

Illustrations by Alicia W. Simon

Editors: Melody Michaux & Dr. Viola McCants Lanier

Gratitude: mother - Viola, father - Danny, daughter - Dr. Viola Mc. Lanier, husband - Lester McCants Sr., sons - Lester Jr. and Joseph McCants, sisters - Beatrice Wynne and Saundra Dancy & Family

ISBN: 978-0-578-38032-2 - Softcover

Printed in the USA   0 2 2 2 2 2

♾This paper meets the requirements of ANSI/NISO Z39.48-1992
(Permanence of Paper)

Margaretfaith1@gmail.com

The Gift of Music & More

To _____

*I want to gift you with this book to make
your heart, mind, and soul sing.*

From _____

Enjoy the Journey

 **Table of Contents**

INTRODUCTION

Thanks to my phenomenal parents, mother, Viola, and father, Danny, who often brought the sounds of music into our home. As young children and teenagers, my awesome older sister, Saundra, and I were singing and dancing in our seats along with other family members to the late 60's and 70's music.

During family gatherings music inspired many of our main events. Good times were experienced with one of my greatest encouragers, my other oldest sister, Beatrice Wynne, and her talented children, Rudy, Liz, Todd, and Cathy. These moments became a wonderful part of fun musical events with her children and other children from the Mitchell Community Center in the Bronx, New York.

With the help of my niece, Liz, I started 3 performance groups that rehearsed and performed at the neighborhood talent shows. These musical groups were "The Soulful Strut's," "The Little Lighters," and "The Psychedelic 4." These were good times in my youthful years. Through my musical entertainment groups, I was recreating what I grew up seeing at the Apollo theatre. My parents took my sister Saundra and I to many unforgettable shows at the amazing Apollo Theatre; and this was an experience that stayed with me.

Though I enjoyed all types of music, my parents made sure that gospel music took the lead on a Sunday morning and other days. More frequently, during the weekday they played rhythm & blues, soul, Motown, and jazz music. We enjoyed visiting the community record store and searching through a selection of various musical genres.   We would happily purchase our favorite songs that consisted of African music, by "Miriam Makeba," gospel music, by "The Mighty Clouds of Joy," jazz music, by Louis Armstrong, Doo-Wop music, by "The Flamingos," reggae music, by Bob Marley, and R&B music, by James Brown.   We couldn't wait to get home and dance to popular songs by The Temptations, The Stylists, The Four Tops, The Supremes, and many more. There were so many songs that I loved, and I am thankful to the radio stations that played the records and introduced us to an array of music. We had no idea that we were experiencing an amazing lifetime of musical memories.

   I thank my parents and I thank you for coming on this musical reflection journey with me as I touch upon some of the outstanding music from Africa to the Present.

Margaret

HOW TO USE THIS BOOK

As you read through this musical book of gratitude, I want you to enjoy humming, tapping your feet, and having a sing-along to the list of talented and creative artists and musicians.

At the top corner of a page, you may see...*Let's Sing*

This page will feature lists of singers and their songs. For each of these pages that list musical artists and a song, I want you to jog-your-memory and *sing* a part of the song that you know. If you don't know it, then feel free and search it. You never know, you might just like it.

At the top corner of a page, you may see...*Poetry in Motion*

This page features spoken words and forms of expression to recognize the impact, the memory, or the times of this music. With music being a form of poetry, it is only fitting to incorporate poems to enhance this musical tribute.

At the top corner of a page, you may see...*Fun with Music*

This is where you will find creative ways to engage in activities that will allow you to reflect on your musical interests and memories. Use this last section of the book to have some musical fun by yourself or with family and friends.

Get ready to enjoy the beauty of the songs that connect you to events that you hold dear in your life.

MUSICAL THOUGHTS

Music is like food for the soul
that transcends all the different races.
It makes you feel good
watching your dancing feet travel to different places.

Songs connect you to memories
gathering your family and friends.
Dance moves we gave names to
repeated again and again.

The instruments combine and create a song
a dance
and a tune.
Go from a thought
to a word,
to a sentence,
to a melody.
It is your music.

Want a reminder of a person?
Play some music.
Want to hear a story?
Play some music
Are you happy?
Play some music.
Forgot the lyrics?
Play the music.
Want to celebrate?
Play that music.

Visit the wonderfulness of musical melodies.
Go through it.
Feel it.
It is your amazing musical world.

Genre

AFRICA

AFRICA

THANK YOU FOR
THE AFRICAN MUSIC

Envision Africa.
Envision the people in the land of Africa.
Envision the movements to the music in Africa.
Envision the shouts of joy to this music in Africa.
Envision the musical significance in its festivals.
Envision the people in their moments of music in religious ceremonies.
Envision wonderful Fatima singing and dancing in her survival.
Envision THIS, in Africa.

African music
and its influence on genres like Jazz, Hip-Hop, and Blues.
African music
and its handcrafted instrumental sounds in sync with powerful beats
that left clues.

It left clues of its people
and where they reside.
Some of these regions in Africa played this music to show their pride.

Curated cultures and various tribes
brought songs, hands claps, rhythmic dance,
and celebrations along the way
using their voices and instruments with an African style
to spread their powerful music through every - day.

REGIONS IN AFRICA & THE MUSICAL ARTISTS

Kenya

J. S. Ondara

Sudan

Rasha

Ethiopia

Teddy Afro

Rawanda

Miss JoJo

Ghana

Rocky Dawuni

Swahili

Ali Kiba

Chad

Matibeye G

Zulu

Sibon Khumala

Nigeria

Fela Sowande

WHO AM I?

I am a South African Singer, Songwriter, Civil Rights Activist, and known as "Mama Africa."
Who Am I? **Miriam Makeba**

I am a Beninese American singer, songwriter, actress, activist, and polyglot who sings and speaks in 8 different languages.
Who Am I? **Angelique Kidjo**

I am a West African singer, actress, women's advocate, and I am known as "The Songbird of Wassoulou."
Who Am I? **Oumou Sangare**

I am a Senegalese singer, songwriter, actor, composer, and politician.
Who Am I? **Youssou N'Dour**

I am Nigerian singer, songwriter, worship leader, and I studied physics at the University of Port Harcourt.
Who Am I? **Osinach Egbu better known as Sinach**

I am a Congolese singer, fashion icon, and I am known as the "King of Rumba Rock"
Who Am I? **Papa Wemba**

I am a South African trumpeter, singer, flugelhornist, composer, and I am known as the "Father of South African Jazz."
Who Am I? **Hugh Masekela**

I am a Nigerian singer, song writer, reggae singer, rapper, dancer, and record label owner.

Who Am I? **Burna Boy**

I am a Nigerian singer, songwriter, actress, and I studied music at Berklee College of Music.

Who Am I? **Tiwa Savage**

I am Ghanaian Afropop singer, reggae artist, and CEO of Burniton Music Group.

Who Am I? **Livingstone E. Satekia better known as Stonebwoy**

They are siblings who sing the hit song "Jerusalema."
Master KG and Nomcebo Zikode

MUSICAL INSTRUMENTS OF AFRICA

FLUTE – a reedless wind instrument known as one of the oldest instruments

DJEMBE – a goblet shaped drum topped with animal skin

MBIRA – a wooden board instrument with attached staggered metal tines

BOLON – a 3 stringed traditional harp

LUTE – a pluckable stringed instrument with a body and neck

KORA – a 21-string instrument with similar features to the lute and harp

NGONI – a wood guitar-like instrument with animal skin draped over it

XYLOPHONE – an instrument with wooden bars that can be struck by using mallets

LAMELLOPHONE – an instrument that consists of a set of lamellae bamboo tongues of different lengths

CLAPSTICKS – similar to drumsticks but used to strike one stick on another

GENRES OF AFRICAN MUSIC

AFROBEAT – consists of the fusion of traditional Nigerian music, jazz, and highlife

APOLA – consists of a percussion-based style of the Muslim Yoruba Nigerian people

ASSIKO – consists of rhythmic dance that developed from Cameroon

BIKUTSI – consists of dance music that developed from the traditional music of Beti in Cameroon

BENGA – consists of popular music using guitars and drum kits from Kenya's capital city of Nairobi

DESERT BLUES – consists of blues music from the people living in the Sahara Desert

CHIMURENGA – uses modern instruments to create the popular music style from Zimbabwe

USING THE LANGUAGES IN AFRICA, HOW DO YOU SAY *"MUSIC?"*

Igbo
"egwu"
means music

Zulu
"umculo"
means music

Shona
"mumhanzi"
means music

Swahili
"muziki"
means music

ADD ON AND SHARE
OTHER AFRICAN MUSIC ARTISTS

1._____
2._____
3._____
4._____
5._____
6._____
7._____
8._____
9._____
10._____

ADD ON AND SHARE
OTHER GOSPEL ARTISTS

1._____
2._____
3._____
4._____
5._____
6._____
7._____
8._____
9._____
10._____

Genre

GOSPEL

THANK YOU FOR THE GOSPEL MUSIC

Gospel music is the foundation of many genres of music. This empowering genre was created with the purpose of helping others to feel connected to God's love, hope, and grace. During slavery, black people would sing gospel songs to promote strength and endurance to get through the daily hardships of being a slave. Used to express feelings of despair or hope, gospel music helped relay messages in the cotton fields of a challenging era.

Today, gospel music continues to be a spiritually enlightening and encouraging part of the black musical experience and is heard through song, seen in dance, and joyfully celebrated with instruments.

Gospel music sings the lyrics of the Gospel
Pouring into the spirit
Telling its story of faith
Telling its story of hope
Telling its story of grace
Telling its story of God
Praying to God
Thanking our God
Oh, how it completes our being with inspiration
With songs of Fatherly love
In songs written and filled with our Gospel

THANK YOU FOR
THE GOSPEL SINGERS

MANY ARE THE KINGS AND QUEENS OF GOSPEL

MAHALIA JACKSON	♪ IF I CAN HELP SOMEBODY ♪
SHIRLEY CAESAR	♪ IT'S ALRIGHT, IT'S OK ♪
MIGHTY CLOUDS OF JOY	♪ MIGHTY HIGH ♪
THE CARAVANS	♪ REMEMBER ME ♪
THE BARRETT SISTERS	♪ WHAT A WONDERFUL WORLD ♪
EDWARD HAWKINS SINGERS	♪ OH HAPPY DAY ♪
ALBERTINA WALKER	♪ JOY WILL COME ♪
THE CLARK SISTERS	♪ BLESSED AND HIGHLY FAVORED ♪
JAMES CLEVELAND	♪ I STOOD ON THE BANK ♪
THE WINANS	♪ AIN'T NO NEED TO WORRY ♪
BEBE WINANS	♪ LAUGHTER IS LIKE A MEDICINE ♪
CECE WINANS	♪ BELIEVE FOR IT ♪
DOROTHY NORWOOD	♪ VICTORY IS MINE ♪
KIRK FRANKLYN	♪ STOMP ♪
ANDRE CROUCH	♪ THOUGH IT ALL ♪

YOLANDA ADAMS	♪ MORE THAN A MELODY ♪
KIM BURREL	♪ I SEE A VICTORY ♪
TYE TRIBETT	♪ VICTORY ♪
HEZEKIAH WALKER	♪ EVERY PRAISE ♪
ISRAEL HOUGHTON	♪ YOU ARE GOOD ♪
MARY MARY	♪ PRAISE YOU ♪
FRED HAMMOND	♪ I WILL TRUST ♪
TASHA COBBS	♪ BREAK EVERY CHAIN ♪
DONNIE MCCLURKIN	♪ STAND ♪
MICHAEL SMITH	♪ WAYMAKER ♪
SMOKIE NORFUL	♪ I NEED YOU NOW ♪
ISRAEL AND THE NEW BREAD	♪ JESUS THE SAME ♪
TAMALA MANN	♪ TAKE ME TO THE KING ♪
TRAVIS GREEN	♪ MADE A WAY ♪
SANACHI	♪ I KNOW WHO I AM ♪
DONALD LAWRENCE	♪ WHEN SUNDAY COMES ♪
LISA P. BROOKS	♪ I WANT TO SAY THANK YOU ♪
EDWIN HAWKINS	♪ IF AT FIRST YOU DON'T SUCCEED ♪

THANK YOU TO THE CHOIRS
& CHOIR LEADERS

THE MISSISSIPPI MASS CHOIR

BROOKLYN TABERNACLE CHOIR

THE LOVE CENTER CHOIR

KIRK FRANKLIN & THE FAMILY

THE THOMPSON COMMUNITY CHOIR

THE MIAMI MASS CHOIR

Poetry in Motion

THANK YOU TO THE PRAISE DANCERS

*The lyrics to the songs sung were expressed through
the praise dance movements.
Feeling the sounds that comes through the instruments
and lends itself to **dance**.
The modern style of music leads the praise dancers' hands, arms,
and feet to gracefully move and **sway**.
And these joy-filled performers express the message of song lyrics
for those who read and those who **pray**.*

Gospel in

FREEDOM

THANK YOU FOR
THE SONGS OF FREEDOM

The creation of freedom songs stems from gospel music and its expressive words describe being free from bondage. These songs were designed to chastise the acts of slavery and racism and its messages sought to encourage liberty and equality.

Slaves sung freedom songs to promote the hope of a better tomorrow and freedom leaders like Harriet Tubman chanted these songs with her followers to keep the momentum of escaping slavery and navigating from the south to the north via the Underground Railroad. The soon to be free slaves were welcomed by some of the helpful white people who opened their homes to those on the song-led freedom journey.

THANK YOU TO
OUR FREEDOM LEADERS

HARRIET TUBMAN

FREDERICK DOUGLAS

SOJOURNER TRUTH

BOOKER T. WASHINGTON

CRISPUS ATTUCKS

THANK YOU FOR
THE FREEDOM SONGS

♪ GO DOWN MOSES ♪
♪ WADE IN THE WATER ♪
♪ SONG OF THE FREE ♪
♪ SWING LOW SWEET CHARIOT ♪
♪ STEAL AWAY ♪
♪ OH, MARY DON'T YOU WEEP ♪
♪ LET US BREAK BREAD TOGETHER ♪
♪ FOLLOW THE DRINKING GOURD ♪
♪ OH FREEDOM ♪
♪ FREEDOM ♪
♪ GET FREE ♪
♪ BIRTHPLACE ♪

ADD ON AND SHARE FREEDOM ARTISTS

1._____
2._____
3._____
4._____
5._____
6._____
7._____
8._____

Genre

BLUES

BEEN AROUND THE BLUES

*If you've been around
you heard the news
of the many great artists
singing the Blues.*

*Stories about heartaches
or hard times is what they use
the bands accompanies them
each instrument playing the Blues.*

*If you've been around
you heard the news
of the many great performers
delivering you that Blues.*

WHO ARE YOU IN THE BLUES?

Albert King – Albert was a blues guitarist who had a musical influence on many guitar players.

♪ I'LL PLAY THE BLUES & DON'T LIE TO ME ♪

Harlan Wolfe – Harlan was a singer with a raspy voice who played the harmonica and the guitar. He is known to be one of the best Chicago artists.

♪ THE RED ROOSTER & HOW MANY MORE YEARS ♪

Muddy Waters – Muddy was known as the father of the modern Chicago Blues. He created a style of his own. He was a songwriter, singer, and musician.

♪ BABY, PLEASE DON'T GO & MANISH B ♪

Ma Rainey – Ma was known as the "Mother of Blues." She was part of the first-generation recording artist of Blues and musically influenced other Blues singers.

♪ PROVE IT ON THE BLUES & BLACK BOTTOM ♪

Charlie Patton – Charlie was known as the "Father of the Delta Blues."

♪ HIGH WATER EVERYWHERE & A SPOONFUL OF BLUES ♪

THANK YOU TO THE BLUES SINGERS

BILLIE HOLIDAY   ♪ GOD BLESS THE CHILD ♪

JELLY ROLL MORTON   ♪ KANSAS CITY STOMP ♪

NAT KING COLE   ♪ SMILE ♪

B.B. KING (LUCILLE)   ♪ MUDDY WATERS" ♪

ROBERT JOHNSON   ♪ SWEET HOME CHICAGO ♪

BESSIE SMITH   ♪ NOBODY KNOWS, EMPRESS OF BLUES ♪

T-BONE WALKER   ♪ CALL IT STORMY MONDAY ♪

BO DIDLEY   ♪ I AM A MAN ♪

BLIND LEMON JEFFERSON
LORRAINE JOHNSON
LESTER YOUNG
LEAD BELLY
NINA SIMONE
WYNTON MARSALIS
ALICE COLTRANE
SARAH VAUGHAN
ROBERT JOHNSON

STANDOUT INSTRUMENTS IN THE DIFFERENT STYLES OF BLUES

Jump blues standout instrument is the horn.
Urban blues music standout instruments
are the drums, guitar, and piano.
Country blues standout instrumental is the fingerstyle guitar.
Boogie Woogie blues music standout instrument is the piano.

ADD ON AND SHARE
OTHER BLUES MUSIC ARTISTS

1._____
2._____
3._____
4._____
5._____
6._____
7._____
8._____
9._____
10._____

Genre

JAZZ

INSTRUMENTS USED IN JAZZ

THANK YOU FOR THE JAZZ

Jazz music is composed of an array of instruments including the trumpet, saxophone, piano, clarinet, bass guitar, and electric guitar. The instrumental ensemble creates melodies that give off a jubilant sound known as jazz.

During the Harlem Renaissance period, jazz clubs were one of the most popular places to listen to music and dance. Though jazz continues to be enjoyed in many places, New Orleans is the city most known for its jazz events and performances.

All that Jazz
Jazz music makes our fingers snap.
Or we tap dance
Tap, Tap, Tap.

THANK YOU TO THE JAZZ MUSICIANS

CAB CALLOWAY ♪ HEIDI HOLMAN ♪

Cab was the leader of one of the biggest bands during the jazz era. He performed through song and dance at the historic "Cotton Club" in Harlem, New York, and donned flashy zoot suits.

LOUIS ARMSTRONG ♪ HELLO DOLLY ♪

Louis was known as the "King of Jazz." As a composer, trumpet player, singer, and an actor, he performed for over 50 years and was also known as "Satchmo."

DIZZY GILLESPIE ♪ LORRAINE ♪

Dizzy was a composer, singer, trumpet player, piano player, and an educator who was known to develop the "bebop" sound.

JOHN COLTRANE ♪ MY FAVORITE THINGS ♪

John was in the forefront of the free jazz movement as a clarinet player, saxophonist and a composer that added the "bebop" sound to his musical delivery.

DUKE ELLINGTON ♪ SATIN DOLL ♪

Duke was a jazz orchestra leader, a pianist, and a composer who adopted the style of jazz-swing- jazz.

CHARLIE PARKER   ♪ NOW'S THE TIME ♪

Charlie was a saxophonist and composer who played fast tempo music using a bebop style.

ELLA FITZGERALD   ♪ A-TISKET-A-TASKIT ♪

Ella was known as the first lady of song and one of the queens of jazz. Her unique speech and impeccable diction gave her voice a sense of pureness.

COUNT BASIE   ♪ APRIL IN PARIS ♪

Count Basie was a composer, a band leader, pianist, and a performer.

MILES DAVIS   ♪ MOON DREAMS ♪

Miles was a trumpet player, singer, bandleader, and composer who is seen as one of the most influential jazz musicians in history.

THANK YOU TO THE JAZZ MUSICIANS

ETTA JAMES
LIONEL HAMPTON
BENNY CARTER
GENE COOPER
TOMMY DORSEY
HERBIE HANCOCK
JIMMY LUNCEFORD
DINAH WASHINGTON
WILTON MARSALIS
COLE HAWKINS
LESTER YOUNG
NAT KING COLE
SARAH VAUGHAN
PEARL BAILEY

ADD ON AND SHARE
OTHER JAZZ MUSIC ARTISTS

1._____
2._____
3._____
4._____
5._____
6._____
7._____
8._____

Genre

DOO-WOP

THANK YOU TO THE DOO-WOP PERFORMERS

Doo-Wop, Doo-Wop, Doo Wop.
Gather the voices together through urban harmony.
A mixture of Gospel and Rhythm & Blues.
Creating a smooth musical sound with voices and instruments.
A mixture of Gospel and Rhythm & Blues.

Snap your hands and tap your feet as you bend down -just a little while
to loosely form "the Doo" and "the Wop."
Take a trip to the 1940's and 1950's to listen to this Doo Wop.
Go from city-to-city and hear the good ole sound of this Doo Wop.
Pop and Rhythm & Blues are the genre sounds taking center place
in this flow of Doo-Wops.
Groups on the corners strategizing to turn a tune
into a harmonizing melody.
It sounds good,
real-good.

THANK YOU TO THE DOO-WOP SINGERS

THE FLAMINGOS	♪ I ONLY HAVE EYES FOR YOU ♪
THE PLATTERS	♪ TWILIGHT TIME ♪
THE CADILLACS	♪ GLORIA ♪
THE COASTER	♪ YAKETY YAK ♪
THE SHIRELLES	♪ MAMA SAID ♪
THE MARCELS	♪ BLUE MOON ♪
THE MOONGLOWS	♪ WE GO TOGETHER ♪
THE DRIFTERS	♪ UNDER THE BOARDWALK ♪
THE CHANTELS	♪ IF YOU TRY ♪
THE CREST	♪ 16 CANDLES ♪
THE FIVE SATINS	♪ A MILLION TO ONE ♪
THE DEL-VIKINGS	♪ BIG BEAT ♪
FRANKIE LYMON	♪ LITTLE BITTY PRETTY ONE ♪

THANK YOU TO THE DOO-WOP MUSICIANS

THE ACCENTS

THE AQUATONES

THE AD LIBB

THE ANGELS

THE ALLEY CATS

THE AVONS

ADD ON AND SHARE OTHER DOO-WOP MUSIC ARTISTS

1._____

2._____

3._____

4._____

5._____

6._____

7._____

8._____

9._____

10._____

Genre

CALYPSO

THANK YOU FOR CALYPSO MUSIC

Calypso music can be traced back to communities of African slaves and is known to stem from Trinidad and Tobago. Evolving from a combination of Spanish, African, French, and English influences, it became a way for people to express themselves in a cheerful and celebratory manner.

Here we come dancing to and fro.
This is the music from the tropical islands.
It's calypso.

Hear the congas, the drums, and the bongos,
the guitars coming together to make a show.
The calypso bands create the island music.
Shake, Shake, Shake.
Up high
and down low.
It's the music.
It is calypso.

THANK YOU TO
THE CALYPSO SINGERS

HARRY BELAFONTE	♪ JUMP IN THE LINE ♪
LOVEY'S STRING BAND	♪ MANGO VERT ♪
LORD MELODY	♪ SI SENOR ♪
DENYSE PLUMMER	♪ FIRE AND STEEL ♪
MIGHTY SPARROW	♪ JEAN AND DINAH ♪
ROARING LION	♪ NETTY NETTY ♪
CALYPSO ROSE	♪ CALYPSO QUEEN ♪
BLINKY & THE ROADMASTERS	♪ CAROLINE ♪
MIGHTY GABBY	♪ JACK ♪
LORD KITCHENER	♪ SUGAR BUM BUM ♪
DAVID RUDDER	♪ CALYPSO MUSIC ♪
ANTHONY JOSEPH	♪ SHINE ♪

CALYPSO MUSIC FACTS

The first calypso song was recorded in 1912 by Lovey's String Band.

The common instruments for calypso music are bongos, timbales, drums, congas, trombones, saxophones, trumpets, bass guitars, electric guitars, or acoustic guitars.

Irving Burgie was one of the greatest song writers of calypso music who composed 34 songs for Harry Belafonte.

Calypso music has been used by politicians to promote political agendas, express the daily struggles of living in Trinidad, and to critique racial and economic inequalities.

ADD ON AND SHARE
OTHER CALYPSO MUSIC ARTISTS

1._____
2._____
3._____
4._____
5._____
6._____
7._____
8._____
9._____
10._____

ADD ON AND SHARE
OTHER REGGAE MUSIC ARTISTS

1._____
2._____
3._____
4._____
5._____
6._____
7._____
8._____
9._____
10._____

Genre

REGGAE

WHO IS THIS REGGAE SINGER?

He is a singer and song writer who was one of the founders of reggae music.
He helped to form the singing group known as "The Wailers."
He is referred to as the "King of Reggae Music."
Bob Marley

He is a music composer and singer.
He is the son of Bob Marley.
He led the family band that released eight studio albums.
Ziggy Marley

He is a lyricist, rapper, and a Jamaican D.J.
He is the youngest son of Bob Marley.
He received four Grammy Awards.
Damian Marley

He was one of Bob Marley's favorite singers.
He is known as "The Crown Prince of Reggae."
Dennis Brown

He is a singer, rapper, and producer, known for performing Dancehall Reggae music.
He was a water polo athlete for a national Jamaican team.
Most of his albums have been nominated for Grammy Awards.
Sean Paul

THANK YOU FOR THE REGGAE MUSIC

Yes…to the Reggae music with something to say
Yes…to the Reggae music that makes you sway

Yes…to the sway of the left hip
Yes…to the sway of the right hip

Yes…to the smooth move of your feet
Oh Yes…to this reggae beat

THANK YOU TO THE REGGAE SINGERS

BOB MARLEY ♪ GET UP STAND UP ♪

ZIGGY MARLEY ♪ LOVE IS MY RELIGION ♪

DESMOND DEKKER ♪ WINGS OF A DOVE ♪

TOOTS AND THE MAYTALS ♪ PRESSURE DROP ♪

PETER TOSH ♪ PICK MYSELF UP ♪

ETANA ♪ SPREAD LOVE ♪

BURNING SPEAR ♪ RED, GOLD AND GREEN ♪

CONSTANTIA MARLEY ♪ PLAY PLAY PLAY ♪

BOB MARLEY & THE WAILERS ♪ 3 LITTLE BIRDS-DON'T WORRY ♪

SIZZLA ♪ THANK YOU MAMA ♪

DENNIS BROWN ♪ LOVE HAS FOUND ITS WAY ♪

DAMIAN MARLEY ♪ THERE FOR YOU ♪

GREGORY ISSACS ♪ NOT THE WAY ♪

FREDDIE MCGREGOR ♪ MOVE UP JAMAICA ♪

TOOTS & MAYTALS ♪ REGGAE GOT SOUL ♪

SOUL MUSIC

THANK YOU FOR THE SOUL MUSIC

Can you describe the evolution of soul music?
Can you describe the soul in this soul music?
Can you express the way it moves your spirit and your soul?
The evolution of soul music inspired, defined, uplifted, curated
and KEPT black people soulful.
The evolution of soul music upraised, empowered, promoted pride
and LOVE in the civil rights era.
It is Soul to Soul with our Soulful Music.

THANK YOU TO THE SOUL SINGERS

ARETHA FRANKLIN   ♪ RESPECT ♪

JAMES BROWN   ♪ SAY IT LOUD, I'M BLACK & I'M PROUD ♪

SAM COOKE   ♪ A CHANGE IS GONNA COME ♪

AL GREEN   ♪ LOVE AND HAPPINESS ♪

TINA TURNER   ♪ PROUD MARY ♪

BARRY WHITE   ♪ PRACTICE WHAT YOU PREACH ♪

OTIS REDDING   ♪ SITTING ON THE DOCK OF THE BAY ♪

JACKIE WILSON   ♪ HIGHER AND HIGHER ♪

WILSON PICKETT   ♪ MUSTANG SALLY ♪

BEN E. KING   ♪ STAND BY ME ♪

CURTIS MAYFIELD   ♪ MOVE ON UP ♪

JANET JACKSON   ♪ CONTROL ♪

RAY CHARLES   ♪ GEORGIA ON MY MIND ♪

PRINCE   ♪ PURPLE RAIN ♪

THE O'JAYS   ♪ I LOVE MUSIC ♪

CURTIS MAYFIELD & THE IMPRESSIONS   ♪ PEOPLE GET READY ♪

STAPLE SINGERS   ♪ FREEDOM HIGHWAY ♪

McFADDEN & WHITEHEAD   ♪ AIN'T NO STOPPING US NOW ♪

MAHALIA JACKSON   ♪ HOW I GOT OVER ♪

FREEDOM SINGERS   ♪ AIN'T GONNA LET NOBODY
TURN US AROUND ♪

THANK YOU TO OUR MUSICAL KINGS, QUEENS, AND LEGENDS

King of Soul
James Brown

King of Pop
Michael Jackson

Queen of Soul
Aretha Franklin

Queen of Rock & Roll
Tina Turner

Legends
Prince
Patty Labelle
Stevie Wonder
Smokey Rob
Ray Charles
Sammy Davis Jr.
The Jackson 5
Janet Jackson
Glady's Knight
Dionne Warwick
The O'Jay's

THANK YOU FOR SUPPORTING THE CIVIL RIGHTS MOVEMENT WITH MUSIC

Oh, how we thank you.
The many who marched and sung with Dr. Martin Luther King Jr.
The many who led civil protests.
The many who connected freedom songs and the journey.
Thank you for moving the path from escape to freedom.
Thank you for Marching On.
Thank you.
From Africa to the Present.

Thank You to the Black Music Action Coalition
A coalition that addressed racism in the music industry.
A coalition that advocated for African Americans.
A coalition that helped discover many talented artists.
A coalition that provided opportunities that led to musical success.

THANK YOU FOR OUR
POPULAR FREEDOM SONGS

We Shall Overcome

One of the most popular songs during civil rights marches

Lift Every Voice

The national black anthem

THANK YOU TO OUR CIVIL RIGHTS ACTIVISTS LEADERS WHO MARCHED AND SUNG

"Yes, we will say their names and remember them forever"

ELLA BAKER

MEDGAR EVERS

ANDREW YOUNG

IDA B. WELLS

CLAUDETTE COLVIN

A. PHILIP RANDOLPH

REVEREND RALPH ABERNATHY

DR. MARTIN LUTHER KING

ROSA PARKS

JAMES FARMER

WHITNEY MOORE YOUNG JR.

JOHN LEWIS

MARCUS GARVEY

STOKELY CARMICHAEL

HOSEA WILLIAMS

REVEREND C.T. VIVIAN

MALCOLM X

ROY WILKINS

FANNIE LOU HAMMER

CORETTA SCOTT KING

NELSON MANDELA

JULIAN BOND

AL SHARPTON

JESSE JACKSON

DESMOND TUTU

ANGELA DAVIS

DAISY BATES

SAMMY DAVIS JR.

ADD ON AND SHARE
OTHER SOUL MUSIC ARTISTS

1._____
2._____
3._____
4._____
5._____
6._____
7._____
8._____
9._____
10._____

ADD ON AND SHARE
OTHER MOTOWN ARTISTS

1._____
2._____
3._____
4._____
5._____
6._____
7._____
8._____
9._____
10._____

"MOTOWN"
SOUL

THANK YOU FOR THE
MOTOWN SOUL MUSIC

Motown legend and founder, Barry Gordy, launched the careers of many musical artists. As an amazing song writer with a big dream, he created a mega memorable musical empire.

Eventually, television followed suit with TV shows that featured Motown and other black performers.

These performers were prepared by legends like Smokey Robinson, who worked diligently with Barry Gordy for many years.

Thank you to the Motown songwriters and producers.

Some of them were Smokey Robinson, Eddie and Brian Holland, Lamont Dozier, Ashford and Simpson, Syreeta Wright, Johnny Bristol, and Ivy Jo Hunter.

Thank you for your songs… "My Girl," "I Heard It Through the Grapevine," "ABC," "How Sweet It Is," "Stop in the Name of Love," "No Where to Run," "I Can't Help Myself," "Reach Out," "I'll be There," and "Fingertips."

Thank you for the house band…The Funk Brothers, Capon Funk, Corey Funk, and Cousin Tyler.

Thank You Motown.

Your music created performers who traveled from town to town delivering soul-filled melodies to crossover audiences.

Audiences that were once separated by the color of skin tones.

Motown's musical shows brought joy to all who were present.

You created a magical moment where the audience appreciation for the music became more important than the differences in skin color.

Thank you, Barry Gordy and everyone involved in the Motown family.

Motown then.

And Motown forever.

THANK YOU FOR THE MOTOWN SOUND

Sensational,
Sharp,
Classy,
Glamorous,
Tailored,
Let's Get ready.
We got ready for the hit songs that brought good times with their sound.
We got ready for the dance moves orchestrated step by step.
Steps taken towards stardom for which they were bound.
And these steps we watched being taken from town to town.
We were ready for Motown.
Let's take it from the top…
The 4 Tops, The Temptations, The Supremes, The Jackson 5, Marvin Gaye, Stevie Wonder, Glady's Knight, Mary Wells, The Marvelettes, Martha & The Vandellas, and The Commodores.

It was Motown's phenomenal sound.

THANK YOU TO THE
SOLO MOTOWN SINGERS

MARVIN GAYE ♪ WHAT'S GOING ON ♪

STEVIE WONDER ♪ I JUST CALLED TO SAY I LOVE ♪

MICHAEL JACKSON ♪ THRILLER ♪

MARY WELLS ♪ MY GUY ♪

JIMMY RUFFIN ♪ WHAT BECOMES OF A BROKEN HEART ♪

EDWIN STARR ♪ TWENTY-FIVE MILES ♪

TAMMI TERRELL ♪ AIN'T NO MOUNTAIN HIGH ENOUGH ♪

SMOKEY ROBINSON ♪ TEARS OF A CLOWN ♪

DIANA ROSS ♪ DO YOU KNOW WHERE YOU'RE GOING TO ♪

LIONEL RICHIE ♪ LADY ♪

THANK YOU TO THE MOTOWN GROUPS

THE TEMPTATIONS	♪ MY GIRL ♪
DIANA ROSS & THE SUPREMES	♪ STOP IN THE NAME OF LOVE ♪
THE FOUR TOPS	♪ REACH OUT ♪
THE JACKSON 5	♪ ABC ♪
SMOKEY ROBINSON & THE MIRACLES	♪ SECOND THAT EMOTION ♪
THE MARVELETTES	♪ MR. POSTMAN ♪
MARTHA REEVES & THE VANDELLAS	♪ DANCING IN THE STREETS ♪
GLADYS KNIGHT & THE PIPS	♪ THAT'S WHAT FRIENDS ARE FOR ♪
THE COMMODORES WITH LIONEL RICHIE	♪ BRICK HOUSE AND SAILING ♪
THE ISLEY BROTHERS	♪ TWIST AND SHOUT ♪
THE CONTOURS	♪ DO YOU LOVE ME ♪
BOYZ II MEN	♪ END OF THE ROAD ♪

THANK YOU TO THE MULTITALENTED CHOREGRAPHERS

SAMMY DAVIS JR.

BILL B. ROBINSON

DEBBIE ALLEN

ALVIN ALLEY

JOSEPHINE BAKER

ARTHUR MITCHELL

KYLE ABRAHAM

GREGORY HINES

MAURICE HINES

KATHERINE DUNHAM

JUDITH JAMISON

GEOFFREY HOLDER

MISTY COPELAND

KYLE ABRAHAM

JUDITH JAMESON

HONI COLES

CHARLES ATKINS

MICHAEL JACKSON

BEYONCE

SAVION GLOVER

DONALD BYRD

ADD ON AND SHARE OTHER BLUES MUSIC ARTISTS & CHOREGRAPHERS

1._____

2._____

3._____

4._____

5._____

6._____

7._____

8._____

Genre

RAP &

HIP HOP

THANK YOU FOR
HIP HOP & RAP MUSIC

It gave a voice to the young people.
It gave a voice to the black experience.
It told stories.
It expressed feelings.
Sometimes beats.
Sometimes without.
It used rhymes to the flow, the raps
That flowed from cool
to slow
to fast
to fierce.
Informing us of each story.
Stories of hardships, happiness, and heroism.
Rap creates creative minds.
Rap, wrapped us in thought.

THANK YOU TO THE
HIP HOP & RAP ARTIST

SUGAR HILL GANG

KANYE WEST

JAY-Z

RUN DMC

SEAN "PUFFY" COMBS

SALT & PEPPER

REMY MA

WILL-I-AM

BIGGIE SMALLS

TUPAC SHAKUR

BUSTA RHYMES

NAS

NICKI MINAJ

RED ALERT

CURTIS "50 CENTS" JACKSON

MACE

RICK ROSS

THANK YOU FOR THE RAP MUSIC

The words speak volumes as they tell the stories that happened.
Say it loud, say it clear; it is the powerful music of rap.
The significance of placing words together to express yourself is
powerful if one can adapt.
In the speaking of your story, your experience, in our soul,
is where we tap.
Traveling through time that takes you from one emotion
to another can take a map.
So, let it be known all around the world about
the amazing music of rap.

THANK YOU TO THE D.J.'S

Thank you to the D.J.'s for playing those songs.
Thank you to the D.J.'s for dancing along.
Thank you to the D.J.'s for bringing the music to the dance floor.
Thank you to the D.J.'s for always leaving us wanting more.

THANK YOU FOR THE RAP & HIP HOP

Dance to the beat, stomp your feet
It's what you do when you hear the Hip Hop beat
The talent is displayed in the music they sing
Keeps you moving,
it's hard to stop some of these things

Wow!

Young people rocking and bopping
Talking all about "What's Hap."
Showing all the creative performers
in a world that never stops.
It's a part of the Hip Hop culture
that is true to its form
Hip-Hop and Rap, continue to go strong.

THANK YOU TO THE
RAP AND HIP-HOP ARTISTS

SUGAR HILL GANG	♪ RAPPERS DELIGHT ♪
BUSTA RHYMES	♪ PUT YOUR HANDS WHERE MY EYES CAN SEE ♪
KOOL AND THE GANG	♪ CELEBRATION ♪
ARRESTED DEVELOPMENT	♪ PEOPLE EVERYDAY ♪
KENDRICK LAMAR	♪ WE GONNA BE ALL RIGHT ♪
SNOOP DOGG	♪ BEAUTIFUL ♪
LIL WAYNE	♪ I PRAY TO THE LORD ♪
DRAKE	♪ GODS PLAN ♪
TUPAC SHAKUR	♪ KEEP YOUR HEAD UP ♪
TONE LOC	♪ WILD THING ♪
NAS	♪ I KNOW I CAN (BE WHAT I WANT TO BE) ♪
QUEEN LATIFAH	♪ UNITY ♪
MISSY ELLIOTT	♪ MUSIC MAKE YOU LOSE CONTROL ♪
PHARRELL WILLIAMS	♪ HAPPY ♪

BIGGIE SMALLS	♪ SKY'S THE LIMIT ♪
CHRIS BROWN	♪ DON'T WAKE ME UP ♪
LL COOL J – SONG	♪ AROUND THE WAY GIRL ♪
DOUGIE FRESH	♪ KEEP RISING TO THE TOP ♪

Poetry in Motion

THE WORDS OF RAP MUSIC

Say it loud, say it clear; it is the powerful music of rap.
In the speaking of your story, your experience, your soul,
guided by hand taps.
The significance of placing words together to express your life
Sometimes happy, sometimes sad, sometimes exciting, sometimes strife.
The map of lyrics takes you on travels from one emotion to another
It's the comradery of musical poetry shared amongst sisters and brothers.

A SPECIAL THANK YOU TO ARRESTED DEVELOPMENT FOR EMBRACING BLACK CULTURE IN THE MUSIC

When you saw Arrested Development perform you encountered a positive pride of black culture and a blended group of men, women, and races who boldly sung, played instruments, and rapped. Their attire was drenched in cultural significance and creative collections. Along with their strong voices, this musical group brought a powerful presence to every stage.

I want to thank, "Speech," also known as Todd Thomas, and his wife Yolanda Thomas, who are longtime friends that have made a personal positive and spiritual impact in my life and the lives of many others.

TENNESSEE

MR. WENDAL

PEOPLE EVERYDAY

REVOLUTION

FISHIN' 4 RELIGION

GIVE A MAN A FISH

EASE MY MIND

RAINING REVOLUTION

NATURAL

MAMA'S ALWAYS ON STAGE

AFRICA'S INSIDE ME

PRIDE

HONEYMOON DAY

THANK YOU TO THE MUSIC PRODUCERS, EXECUTIVES, MANAGERS, & FOUNDERS

These professionals have made an impact on many music artists careers, great contributions to the musical world, are well accomplished, multitalented, and some are legendary and Grammy Award winners.

Quincy Jones: Music producer, songwriter, composer, musician, music arranger

Barry Gordy: Music producer, song writer and music legend who founded Motown record label company

Gamble and Huff: Music producers, song writer, and developed the Philadelphia soul music genre of the 1970s

Smoky Robinson: Motown executive, producer, singer, songwriter

Rodney Jenkins: Record producer, songwriter, rapper

Bobby Robinson: Independent music producer, legendary record shop owner in Harlem, NY

Dr. Dre: Music producer, rap artist, CEO of Aftermath Entertainment

Timbaland: Music producer, songwriter, singer, rap artist

Sean Combs: Music producer, Hip Hop artist, music executive, founder of Bad Boy Records

Jay-Z: Music executive, rap artist, media proprietor

Babyface: Music producer, executive, singer, song writer and co-founder of LaFace Records

La Reid: Music producer, song writer, and cofounder of LaFace Records

Jermaine Dupree: Music executive, song writer, DJ, rap artist, Head of So So Def Records

Missy Elliott: Music producer, songwriter, singer, rapper

Master P: Music executive, rap artist, founder of No Limit Records

50 cent: Music producer, rap artist, leader of G Unit

Teddy Riley: Music producer, singer, song writer, creator of new jack swing genre

Yandy Smith Harris: Music producer, manager

Pebbles: Music Producer, song writer, singer

ADD ON AND SHARE OTHER
HIP HOP ARTISTS & PRODUCERS

1._____
2._____
3._____
4._____
5._____
6._____
7._____
8._____
9._____
10._____

Genre

RHYTHM
& BLUES

THANK YOU FOR THE RHYTHM AND BLUES

Welcome to the awesome world of R&B.
Smooth, talented, classy singers, is what you will see.
If you have experienced being in their audience,
you must have been filled with glee.
The presentation of their songs
is quite something to see
Those artists don't just sing
They "saaaannnng" that R&B.

Hello there people,
Have you heard the news?
Some of the best music is called
Rhythm and Blues.
Sing on- sing on, sing on, sang.

We followed along and sang the songs.
Perhaps a little off beat sometimes,
or with a few added words.
But our hearts
and our memories were
in it.
I mean Really
in it.
Real Good Music.
With Really Good Times.

THANK YOU TO THE R&B SINGERS

ISAAC HAYES	♪ NEVER CAN SAY GOODBYE ♪
PRINCE	♪ PURPLE RAIN ♪
JANET JACKSON	♪ CONTROL ♪
MARY J. BLIGE	♪ WHAT'S THE 411 ♪
BEYONCÉ	♪ CRAZY IN LOVE ♪
DESTINY'S CHILD	♪ SURVIVOR ♪
SWV	♪ WEAK ♪
XSCAPE	♪ JUST KICKIN' IT ♪
TINA TURNER	♪ PROUD MARY ♪
AL GREEN	♪ LOVE AND HAPPINESS ♪
ETTA JAMES	♪ AT LAST ♪
PEARL BAILEY	♪ HELLO DOLLY ♪
EMOTIONS	♪ YOU GOT THE BEST OF MY LOVE ♪
LUTHER VANDROSS	♪ DANCE WITH MY FATHER ♪
CHUCK JACKSON	♪ ANY DAY NOW ♪
USHER	♪ YEAH ♪
ALICIA KEYS	♪ A WOMEN'S WORTH ♪

TONI BRAXTON	♪ UN-BREAK MY HEART ♪
BABYFACE	♪ THIS IS FOR THE COOL IN YOU ♪
CHAKA KHAN	♪ TELL ME SOMETHING GOOD ♪
KEITH SWEAT	♪ RIGHT AND WRONG ♪
BARRY WHITE	♪ MY FIRST, MY LAST ♪
NEW EDITION	♪ CANDY GIRL ♪
ENVOGUE	♪ HOLD ON ♪
JOHN LEGEND	♪ ORDINARY PEOPLE ♪
JODECI	♪ COME AND TALK TO ME ♪
PATTI LABELLE	♪ IF ONLY YOU KNEW ♪
ROBERTA FLACK	♪ THE FIRST TIME EVER I SAW YOU FACE ♪
BRANDY	♪ BABY ♪
TLC	♪ WATERFALLS ♪
MONICA	♪ DON'T TAKE IT PERSONAL ♪
ASHFORD & SIMPSON	♪ SOLID AS A ROCK ♪
LAUREN HILL	♪ READY OR NOT ♪
PEABO BRYSON	♪ A WHOLE NEW WORLD ♪
PHYLISS HYMAN	♪ BETCHA BY GOLLY WOW ♪
STYLISTICS	♪ STOP, LOOK, LISTEN ♪
BLACKSTREET	♪ NO DIGGITY ♪
MISSY ELLIOTT	♪ MUSIC MAKES YOU LOSE CONTROL ♪
KOOL AND THE GANG	♪ CELEBRATION ♪

CHUBBY CHECKER	♪ THE TWIST ♪
HARRY MELVIN & THE BLUE NOTES	♪ WAKE UP EVERBODY ♪
WHITNEY HOUSTON	♪ THE GREATEST LOVE ♪
BILL WITHERS	♪ LEAN ON ME ♪
STEPHANIE MILLS	♪ HOME ♪
JILL SCOTT	♪ A LONG WALK ♪
MARIAH CAREY	♪ HERO AND WHEN YOU BELIEVE ♪
MCFADDEN & WHITEHEAD	♪ AIN'T NO STOPPING US NOW ♪
CYNTHIA ERIVA –SONG	♪ STAND UP ♪
DELFONICS	♪ LA-LA MEANS I LOVE YOU ♪
BLUE MAJIC	♪ THREE RING CIRCUS ♪
FANTASIA	♪ I BELIEVE ♪
ERYKAH BADU	♪ ON AND ON ♪
BABYFACE	♪ SOMEONE TO LOVE ♪
FAITH EVANS	♪ SOON AS I GET HOME ♪
KEM	♪ LOVE NEVER FAILS ♪
ASHANTI	♪ HAPPY ♪
THE SPINNERS	♪ ROCKIN' ROBIN ♪
EARTH, WIND, AND FIRE	♪ REASONS ♪
BRIAN MCNIGHT	♪ BACK AT ONE ♪
BILLY PAUL	♪ AM I BLACK ENOUGH FOR YOU ♪
RIHANNA	♪ UMBRELLA ♪

THANK YOU TO THE MULTICULTURAL SINGERS & DANCERS

FRANK SINATRA ♪ NEW YORK ♪

TONY BENNETT ♪ THE GOOD LIFE ♪

JOE COCKER ♪ YOU ARE SO BEAUTIFUL ♪

THE BEATLES ♪ LET IT BE ♪

BARRY MANILOW ♪ I MADE IT THROUGH THE RAIN ♪

BARBARA STREISAND ♪ THE WAY WE WERE ♪

BRUCE SPRINGSTEEN ♪ THIS LAND IS YOUR LAND ♪

PAUL MCCARTNEY ♪ EBONY & IVORY ♪

ELTON JOHN ♪ CROCODILE ROCK ♪

GEORGE HARRISON ♪ MY SWEET LORD ♪

CELINE DION ♪ MY HEART WILL GO ON ♪

BONNIE RAITT ♪ CAN'T MAKE YOU LOVE ME ♪

TEENA MARIE ♪ OOH LA LA LA ♪

ANNIE LENNOX ♪ WHY ♪

Let's Sing

OSMONDS	♪ ONE BAD APPLE ♪
BOY GEORGE	♪ DO YOU REALLY WANT TO HURT ME ♪
BEE GEES	♪ MORE THAN A WOMAN ♪
MENUDO	♪ IF YOU'RE NOT HERE ♪
JOSE FELICIANO	♪ CALIFORNIA DREAMING ♪
LINKIN PARK	♪ NUMB ♪
THE ROLLING STONES	♪ SHE'S A RAINBOW ♪
PAULA ABDUL	♪ STRAIGHT UP ♪
JOAN BAEZ	♪ WE SHALL OVERCOME ♪
TOM JONES	♪ IT'S NOT UNUSUAL ♪
JENNIFER LOPEZ	♪ LOVE DON'T COST A THING ♪
KELLY CLARKSON	♪ SINCE U BEEN GONE ♪
BACKSTREET BOYS	♪ EVERYBODY ♪
JUSTIN TIMBERLAKE	♪ CRY ME A RIVER ♪
ADELE	♪ SOMEONE LIKE YOU ♪
CASS ELLIOT	♪ CALIFORNIA DREAMIN' ♪
NSYNC	♪ THIS I PROMISE YOU ♪
BRUNO MARS	♪ TALKING TO THE MOON ♪
DOLLY PARTON	♪ 9 TO 5 ♪

MADONNA ♪ VOGUE ♪

BRUNO MARS ♪ TALKING TO THE MOON ♪

PINK ♪ TRY ♪

LADY GAGA ♪ BORN THIS WAY ♪

VANILLA ICE ♪ ICE ICE BABY ♪

ARIANA GRANDE ♪ 7 RINGS ♪

ADD ON AND SHARE OTHER R & B & MULTICULTURAL ARTISTS

1._____
2._____
3._____
4._____
5._____
6._____
7._____
8._____
9._____
10._____

MUSICAL

TELEVISION

SHOWS

THANK YOU FOR THE MUSIC ON TELEVISION

There were some soul-filled songs coming from
"The Apollo Theatre."
There were
super stellar voices coming
"The Flip Wilson Show."
We could break out in a dance
when watching
"American Band Stand."
Or maybe we just hummed the tune
when admiring the talent on
"American Idol."

We sung the music.
We shared the music.
We watched the music.
We danced to the music.

THANK YOU FOR
THE APOLLO THEATRE

A special Thank You to the legendary Apollo Theatre located in Harlem, New York on 125th street. This theatre was a lifetime experience that provided exposure to a multitude of musical genres in the black community.

Upon opening its doors in 1913, the Apollo Theatre played a key role in the Harlem Renaissance era.

It played a major role in bringing black talent to the forefront.

It played a major role in recognizing black success.

When you heard the applause, you knew the singer was great.

When you heard the applause, you knew the dancer was great.

When you they laughed at the jokes, you knew the comedian was great.

When you went to Amateur Hour night, you knew a star was among them.

There was so much greatness that came from the legendary Apollo theatre.

Thank You to the Apollo Theatre

THANK YOU FOR
THE ED SULLIVAN SHOW

On Sunday evening you can catch the musical Ed Sullivan Show. From 1948 to1971, it was hosted by Ed Sullivan himself.

The majority of guests were Caucasian, along with the host.

However, he was one of the first and few hosts who presented black performers on his show.

Some of those musical artists were: Harry Belafonte, Nat King Cole, Ella Fitzgerald, Louis Armstrong, Bill "Bojangles" Robinson, and Diane Carroll.

Ed Sullivan had a great appreciation for the Motown sound created by mogul Barry Gordy.

He appreciated entertainers like the Supremes, The Four Tops, The Temptations, and other Motown singers.

However, Ed was threatened for highlighting and presenting black performers.

Yet, the host and humanitarian, Ed Sullivan, continued to do what was right for all people because he appreciated good music.

Because of his actions, the Ed Sullivan Show was a great part of the Civil Rights Movement.

He continuously gave accolades to many talented black performers.

Years later, Ed Sullivan's granddaughter, Margo Speciale, and Diane Carroll's daughter, Suzanne Kay, worked in partnership to create a document highlighting his impact on the civil rights movement.

Thank You to the Ed Sullivan Show

THANK YOU FOR
THE SOUL TRAIN SHOW

For 35 years, we were entertained by the Soul Train music television show.

Once each week this show brought a multitude of talented performers and creative dancers into homes.

Many of us looked forward to watching Soul Train Dancers form the famous Soul Train line.

This popular formation consisted of people lining up in two lines, facing each other, and dancing down the aisle together; solo or in twos.

We pay homage to Don Cornelius for creating this musical production.

As the executive producer, Mr. Cornelius sported a well-groomed large Afro and tailored sharp suits. His style was second to none.

The genres of music presented on the show were disco, R&B, hip hop, gospel, jazz, and many more.

Gladys Knight and the Pips were the first entertainers on this show.

Some of the other highlighted artists were Jackson 5, Freddy Jackson, Wyclef Jean, Millie Jackson, The Isley Brothers, the Spinners, Al Jarreau, K. C. and the Sunshine Band, Earth, Wind, & Fire, Elton John, Chaka Khan, B.B. King, M.C. Hammer and Maxwell.

Some of the well-known dancers were Damita Jo Freeman, Gerald Brown, Terry Brown, Judy Jones, Patricia Williamson, Denise Smith, and Hollis Pippin.

Soul train brought fun into dancing and feeling the joy of music.

Thank you to the Soul Train Music Show

THANK YOU TO THE
BLACK ENTERTAINMENT
TELEVISION AWARDS

Created in1980, the Black Entertainment Television (BET) network honored black people and provided a forum for recognition of black creative work and entertainment.

The stage of the BET awards opened the door to black entertainers presenting their talent.

It gave a voice to honor everyday people and people in the entertainment industry.

Music played an intricate part of the BET award shows and several musical entertainers received the opportunity to be honored because of BET.

Every year our phenomenal first black president, Barack Obama, and our elegant First Lady, Michelle Obama hosted a musical tribute at the white house.

In 2016, BET presented the "Love and Happiness" musical celebration for Barack and Michelle Obama, which consisted of performances that included many different genres.

Thank you to the founders, Robert L. Johnson and Sheila Johnson, for providing a platform for black entertainers.

Much gratitude is given to Steven Hill, President of Programming, and Deborah Lee, CEO of BET, who worked diligently to highlight people of color in the entertainment industry.

Thank you to the BET Network

MUSIC
IN THE
COMMUNITY

A HAIKU
Dancing to and fro
feel the breeze across the floor
fresh air in the steps

AN ALLITERATION
Music marvels miraculously through the
masterpiece of songs and dance.
May you major in marvelous music of some sort everyday!

A RHYME
Gospel music is great inspiration
messages of faith, hope, love, and prasies across the nation.
Songs about victories, sacrifices, and testimonies
are topped off with determination.
Gospel music fuels our beings and brings about a revelation.

AN ONAMONAPIA
Drip drops of musical notes
can come together to make a splash
across the pages of songwriters.

MUSIC IN THE SCHOOLS

Many valuable lessons were learned though the messages in songs. The ABC song, counting songs and songs like "If Your Happy and You Know It," teaches sequences, following directions, and allows for musical participation in the early years. School system performing arts programs include student singers, dancers, poets, and musicians. Bands, choirs, and dance classes were instrumental courses for teaching the arts. Performing arts teachers worked diligently to enhance the talent that many students possessed; and I, Margaret McCants, was one of those teachers who led the performance arts program.

Public School 85 in the Bronx, New York
In the annual black history plays, we created an ensemble of performances that included dramatic speeches, singing, and dancing.

I.S. 137 in the Bronx, New York
As another way to teach black culture, we created several productions to show the journey from Africa to the present. Our musical multicultural performances included dance, sharing, and songs from across many lands.

Coretta Scott King Middle School in Atlanta, Georgia
To continue bringing black history musical plays to the schools, we used music from different genres to show the journey from Africa to the present.

THANK YOU TO THE PERFORMING FAMILY AND FRIENDS

LESTER MCCANTS SR.

LESTER MCCANTS JR.

VIOLA MCCANTS LANIER

JAMES LANIER

JOHN BROWN JR.

JOSEPH MCCANTS

MARGARET MCCANTS

CHRISTOPHER LANIER

MAYA MCCANTS

LEAH MCCANTS

BRIE MCCANTS

LAMONT MCCANTS

LARICE MCCANTS

CATHY WYNNE

TODD WYNNE

JAMES WYNNE

SHANIQUE JOHNSON

DANASIA DANCY

ALAYA WYNNE

SPENCER BROWN

RONALD MARSHALL

MIRIAM MILLER

RENEL MARSHALL

TROY JOHNSON RIP

WAYNE RICHARDSON

SUMMER MORGAN

SUMEKO DOWNS

DARYL DANCY

DAN BROWN

TONY MICHAUX

MELODY MICHAUX

ALLISON MCGEE

MYA MCGEE

KEVIN LIGHTBURN

PAM LIGHTBURN

AC CHEEKS

GALE CHEEKS

MARV RICHARDSON

THURSTIN DONALD

DELINDA ENRIQUES

NICK ENRIQUES JR.

ROSE VOKHIWA

ABBY GONZALEZ

CHERYL JOHNSON

MELISSA ENRIQUES

RICKY GOMEZ

CORY GOMEZ

BRIE MCCANTS

RONALD MARSHALL

RENEL MARSHALL

TROY JOHNSON

WAYNE RICHARDSON

RICKY GOMEZ

CORY GOMEZ

THANK YOU FOR YOUR MUSICAL PERSPECTIVE CHILDREN

*Christopher say's "I appreciate many genres of music.
I connect most with Hip-Hop and R&B.
Making music makes me feel good."*

*Lamont say's "I enjoy listening to music and sometimes dancing.
My favorite types of music are R&B and Hip-Hop."*

*Grand girl Mya McCants says, "I enjoy music.
I like the beats and the sounds. It makes me feel happy.
I love to dance and sing."*

*Grand girl Leah McCants says, "Music makes me feel good.
Music makes me feel happy.
I like to put on shows for my family. I love to dance and sing."*

*Grand girl Brie McCants says, "I like music.
I like having fun with music."*

You-go Grands..

THANK YOU TO THE MUSICAL ARTIST IN THE COMMUNITIES

From the churches
From the cancer support groups
You Performed with Power.

From Producing Music
And Recording Videos
You Performed with Power.

From the "Africa to the Present" Play
And the Singing groups

You Performed with Power.

You have impacted our communities.
And YOU have infused your Musical Power.

THANK YOU TO THE CHURCH & COMMUNITY MUSICAL ARTISTS WITH POWER IN THEIR VOICES

FELICIA ROGERS

SHERWIN MACKINTOSH

STEVE JOHNSON

DARYL DANCY

MIKE PATTERSON

BYRON WORD

ANTHONY PETTY

BEVERLY CHERRY

DANIELLE WORD

JODIE (RIP)

SUMMER "ONESUMZ" MORGAN

SHAMICHAEL CHASTAIN TRAYLOR

SHEILA GALILEE

NEISHA HILLARD

SEPHRA GERALD

ADWOWA ANNAN

DANIELLE HALL WILLS

TERRENCE GOLDEN

SPOTLIGHT ON THE MUSICAL COMMUNITY GROUPS

As children, these family members and friends showed their creative and musical talents through song and dance groups. Thank you to sis Bea, Ms. Isabel, and all the parents for their wonderful support during those early years.

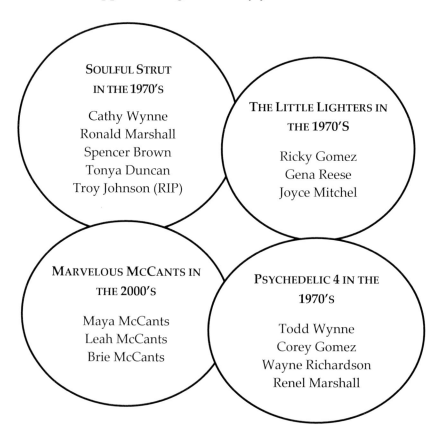

SOULFUL STRUT IN THE 1970'S

Cathy Wynne
Ronald Marshall
Spencer Brown
Tonya Duncan
Troy Johnson (RIP)

THE LITTLE LIGHTERS IN THE 1970'S

Ricky Gomez
Gena Reese
Joyce Mitchel

MARVELOUS MCCANTS IN THE 2000'S

Maya McCants
Leah McCants
Brie McCants

PSYCHEDELIC 4 IN THE 1970'S

Todd Wynne
Corey Gomez
Wayne Richardson
Renel Marshall

AUDIO DEVICES

THE EVOLUTION OF AUDIO DEVICES

78' Album

45' Record

Tape Cassette

Eight Track Tape

Compact Disc

MP3 Player

Smart Phone

MUSICAL PLAYS

THANK YOU FOR
THE MUSICAL PLAYS

The Lion King

It Captures
the movement
the culture
the costumes
and the dance.
It Captures
the hope
the pride
the triumph
and a born to be king who gets a second chance.

The Wiz

Oh, what a musical
to travel with a brown skin Dorothy,
and her companions
to the land of Oz.
On the yellow brick road
as they search and journey for what they already possessed inside.

Color Purple

A young girl
experiencing hard times
yearning for her sister
and journeying through the Blues
in a story that displays discourse plus love
and the family that we choose.

Mama I Wanna Sing

A preacher's daughter
Just wanting to sing songs
With a sister who later told the story
of the fame that later came along.

THANK YOU FOR
THE TYLER PERRY PLAYS

From
I Know I've Been Changed
to "I Can Do Bad All by Myself"

From "Diary of a Mad Black Woman"
to "Why Did I Get Married"

From "What's Done in the Dark"
to "Laugh To Keep From Crying"

A King of plays
Filled with black entertainers.
Sporting leading roles.
His name is Tyler Perry.
His dream of providing the black community with a space and place for
being recognized for their talent, their voice, and their presence.

*His name is **Tyler Perry**.*
We thank you.

MUSICAL
ACTIVITIES

MUSIC MOMENTS

Use the information in this book as a reference to list 2 songs from each genre

African Music

_____

_____

Gospel

_____

_____

Blues

_____

_____

Jazz

_____

_____

Calypso

_____

_____

Reggae

_____

_____

Soul "Motown" & Rhythm and Blues

_____

_____

Rap

_____

_____

Hip Hop

_____

_____

Rhythm & Blues

_____

_____

MUSICAL LYRICS

Jog your memory and fill in the rest of the song lyric.

1. Make this world a better place

   _____

2. We'll walk hand and hand

   _____

3. You know we've got to find a way to bring some

   _____

4. Teach them well and let them

   _____

5. I worked on jobs with my feet

   _____

6. It's been a long time but

   _____

7. Reach out and touch

   _____

8. Say it loud

   _____

9. Lord lift us up where

    _____

10. Sing a song full of the faith

    _____

11. It's been a long time coming but

    _____

12. Is it worth it? Let me

    _____

13. I'm starting with the man in the mirror

    _____

14. Concrete jungle where dreams are made of

    _____

15. Don't worry about a thing cause

    _____

MATCH THE LYRICS TO THE SONGS

Lyrics	Songs
• They're dancing on the street	A. I Feel Good
• And somewhere on the way you might find out who you are	B. Soul Power
• Sit yourself down in a car and take a ride, and while you're moving	C. Respect
• Huh, we want it	D. Get on the Good Foot
• It's growing in the street right through the creek	E. Living in America
• All I'm asking for is a little respect	F. Rock Steady
• When evening falls so hard I will comfort you	G. Think
• Huh, I got soul	H. Spanish Harlem
• And I feel nice, like sugar and spice	I. Super Bad
• About the good things I've done for you	J. A Bridge Over Troubled Waters

MUSIC DURING EVENTS

The music is used to create an ATMOSPHERE.

The music is used to encourage PARTICIPATION.

The music is used to set the SCENE.

The music is used to ENTERTAIN.

What events have you went to or participated in
that was full of music?

_____

_____

_____

_____

_____

_____

_____

_____

THANK YOU FOR THE MUSIC THAT ADDS AN IMPACT TO THE MOVIES

List 3 children movies that are filled with music.

_____

_____

_____

List 3 adult movies that are filled with music.

_____

_____

_____

MUSICAL MEMORIES

Name 2 musical events that you were a part of as a child.

Which 2 musical shows would you like to be a part of?
Would you want to be the lead actor or supporting actor?

Musical Show	Musical Show
Lead Actor or Supporting Actor?	Lead Actor or Supporting Actor?

Which 2 songs do you like to dance to?

♪ _____

♪ _____

Which 2 performing groups would you like the chance to perform with?

♪ _____

♪ _____

Who are the 2 singers that you would like to do a duet with?

♪ _____

♪ _____

What are your 2 favorite bands?

♪ _____

♪ _____

Who are your 2 favorite song writers?

♪ _____

♪ _____

Who are your 2 favorite Disc Jockey's (D.J.'s)?

♪ _____

♪ _____

What are the 2 topics that you would like to write a song about?

♪ _____

♪ _____

What is the name of your 2-favorite family-related songs?

♪ _____

♪ _____

Which 2 songs do most people consider as inspirational?

♪ _____

♪ _____

Which 2 songs can get almost the entire party on the dance floor?

♪ _____

♪ _____

What are your 2 favorite songs that brings back memories ?

♪ _____

♪ _____

Which 2 songs makes your heart smile?

♪ _____

♪ _____

Which 2 songs makes you feel empowered?

♪ _____

♪ _____

Which 2 artists would you want to perform at your birthday party?

♪ _____

♪ _____

Fun with Music

What are the 2 musical instruments that you would like to learn how to play?

♪ _____

♪ _____

Which 2 musical instruments do you know how to play?

♪ _____

♪ _____

What are your 2 favorite musical movies?

♪ _____

♪ _____

Name one performer that you have seen in concert and name one that you would like to see.

♪ _____

♪ _____

THERE IS A SONG
INSIDE OF ALL OF US

Write a song about you.

_____

_____

_____

_____

_____

_____

_____

_____

_____

_____

_____

_____

_____

_____

_____

_____

_____

_____

_____

_____

_____

_____

_____

_____

_____

_____

NAME A SONG THAT...

Makes you want to dance:

♪ _____

Inspires you:

♪ _____

Reminds you that you are loved:

♪ _____

Increases your faith:

♪ _____

Make you feel like a child again:

♪ _____

Makes you love the skin that you are in:

♪ _____

Makes you feel powerful:

♪ _____

Makes you appreciate your family:

♪ _____

Makes you joyful:

♪ _____

Reminds you of your friends:

♪ _____

GREAT GENRES, GREAT MUSIC

For each genre of music, list a song, the artist, and the type of instrument heard within that song.

GENRE	SONG TITLE	SINGER(S)	INSTRUMENTS
African			
Gospel			
Freedom			
Blues			
Jazz			
Calypso			
Reggae			
Soul			
Rhythm & Blues			
Rap			
Hip Hop			

FAMILY FUN WITH MUSICALS

Have fun with family and for each of the movie musicals listed below write down your parent's and/or grandparent's favorite part of the movie.

FAMILY MEMBER NAME	FAVORITE MOMENT

Dream Girls

The Five Heartbeats

The Temptations

The Wiz

What's Love Got to Do It

MOVING WITH MOTOWN

List your favorite Motown songs and the singer (s).

FIT THE GENRE

Write the genre of music for each musical artist below.

Desmond Dekker	Louie Armstrong
_____	_____

Mahalia Jackson	Nat King Cole
_____	_____

Aretha Franklin	Angelique Kidjo
_____	_____

MC Hammer	Speech Thomas
_____	_____

Ray Charles	Shirley Ceasar
_____	_____

Stevie Wonder
_____

B.B. King
_____

James Brown
_____

Miriam Makeba
_____

Mary J. Blige
_____

Michael Jackson
_____

Sam Cooke
_____

Glady's Knight
_____

Tina Turner
_____

Dougie Fresh
_____

Lord Melody
_____

Thank You

for going on this Musical Journey

From Africa to the Present

ABOUT THE AUTHOR

As I write throughout my chemotherapy treatment, I am thankful to Amazing PA Allison Bryant, Dr. Godbee, and their team at CTCA in Georgia. And of course, thankful for many Prayers and Church. I let the joy of music wonderfully stir my soul. My life experiences have consisted of many types of music, from African, to Gospel, to Jazz, to the Blues, to Caribbean, to Reggae, to Soul, to Motown, to Rap and Rhythm & Blues. My interest in the different musical genres grew from the love of my parents taking me to the legendary Apollo Theatre. This Apollo Theatre broke barriers in putting forth so many talented music artists.

Though the black community sits amid some trials and tribulations, we can go back, time and time again, to the hopeful lyrics and the many songs, such as "We Shall Overcome," and

"Ain't No Stoppin' Us Now." We sit amongst many victories thanks to our great leaders from the past who gallantly marched, protested, spoke, and sang songs of wisdom, hope, knowledge, and determination.

To this day I enjoy dancing and singing to the music played from Africa to this present time, with gospel music being one of my favorite genres.

I'm thankful to my daughter, Dr. Viola Lanier, retired school principal Melody Michaux, retired art teacher, Alicia Williams-Simon, and other family and friends for their support.

Thank you for enjoying this book. Continue to look forward to the dynamic PLAY and the NEXT BOOK "From AFRICA to the PRESENT."

Margaret Jenkins McCants